PAPER QUILLING GUIDE

THE ESSENTIAL STEP BY STEP GUIDE ON LEARNING THE SKILLS AND TECHNIQUES TO MAKING AMAZING QUILLING WORKS WITH 12 QUILLING PROJECTS

MICHELLE PIERCE

Made with ♥ on the Notion Press Platform
www.notionpress.com

Contents

Title Page

PAPER QUILLING GUIDE

The essential step by step guide on learning the skills and techniques to making amazing quilling works with 12 quilling projects

Michelle Pierce

CHAPTER ONE

INTRODUCTION TO QUILLING

What is Quilling?

Quilling, the curling and molding of thin paper strips to make a good design, has been around for a considerable length of time — hundreds, truth be told. During the Renaissance, nuns and priests would move gold-overlaid paper leftovers tended to during the bookmaking cycle, and use them to enliven strict articles as an option in contrast to exorbitant gold filigree. Quilling later turned into a diversion of eighteenth and nineteenth century youngsters in England, who might finish service trays and household items with paper filigree. The training crossed the Atlantic with pioneers, who added quilling to light sconces and plate as home enhancements or decorations.

In the entirety of that time, the cycle has stayed particularly the equivalent, however quilling plans and claim to fame supplies have unquestionably gotten up to speed to the 21st century. Today a few fans center around making unfathomably point by point 3-D figures, while others favor divider measured gallery establishments. Maybe quilling is most popular, however, as a method of carrying character to high quality cards.

The short rundown of necessities incorporates portions of lightweight paper, stick, and an apparatus with which to roll the paper — that is it! Far and away superior, there's likely no compelling reason to search for provisions before you have a go at quilling, as a bamboo stick, round toothpick, or even a cake analyzer from your kitchen cabinet can fill in as a substitute device. Cut your own training takes from a sheet of normal PC paper, utilizing a paper shaper.

Numerous expressions and artworks stores sell essential devices and bundles of multicolor paper strips. Wonderful papers and other quilling supplies are accessible from online providers. Gracious, and ultimately, one prerequisite that is not accessible for procurement, yet will likewise be required, is a considerable measure of tolerance. With a little practice, in any case, I can nearly anticipate you'll discover quilling to be imaginatively fulfilling and fun.

Before you start quilling, in here is all that you have to think about quilling. Quilling or paper filigree is a work of art that includes the utilization of portions of paper that are rolled, molded, and stuck together to make ornamental plans.

With assistance of quilling you can make keyrings, gems, enlivening things, Greeting cards, 3D models and substantially more thing. In this book you can figure out how to begin with quilling, making essential shapes, making keyring, ornamental things, bloom and furthermore some fundamental information about quilling. I likewise included loads of photographs for simple comprehension.

CHAPTER TWO

THE BASICS OF PAPER QUILLING

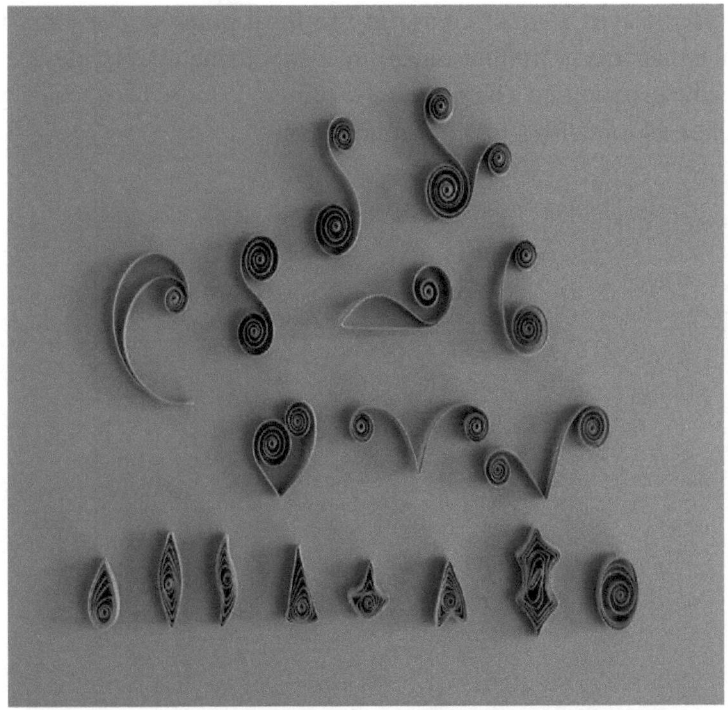

The tasks in this guide highlight the tear loop, yet there are numerous other fascinating shapes to attempt — marquises, sharpened stones, holly leaves, and a wide range of lovely parchments, just to give some examples.

Materials:

Quilling paper: 1/8″, standard width

Quilling device needle apparatus or opened instrument

Ruler

Scissors

Tweezers

Glue clear-drying, reasonable for paper

Plastic top to use as a glue palette

T-pin, paper penetrating apparatus, or round toothpick

Glass-head straight pins

Non-stick work board, stopper, or styrofoam something into which you can stick pins

Damp material to keep fingers liberated from stick

Guidelines:

When buying an instrument there are 2 essential sorts: an opened device and needle device. The opened device is simplest to utilize; its lone burden is that the space leaves a small crease in the focal point of the loop. On the off chance that this is troublesome, buy a super fine opened device or attempt a needle instrument. The needle instrument is more hard to ace, yet the prize will be a loop with a totally round focus.

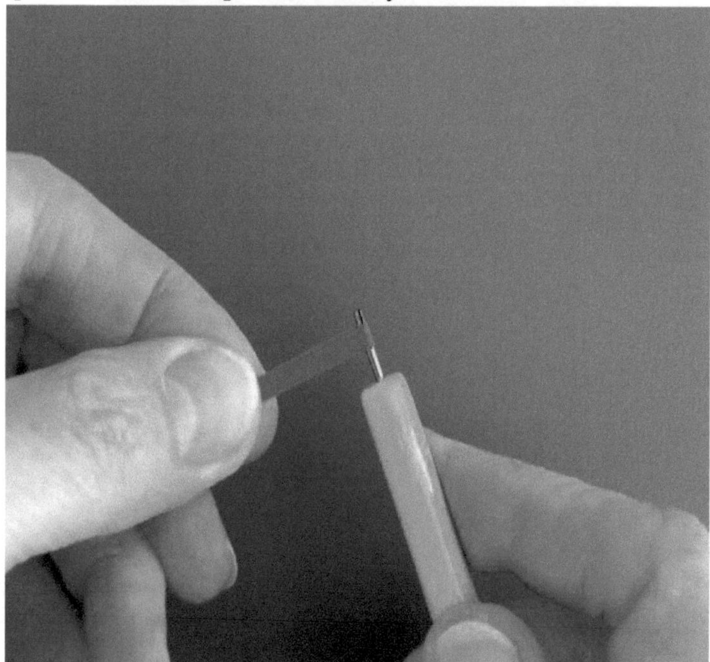

To roll a curl with an opened apparatus: Slide the finish of a strip into the space, and turn the device with one hand while uniformly managing the strip with the other.

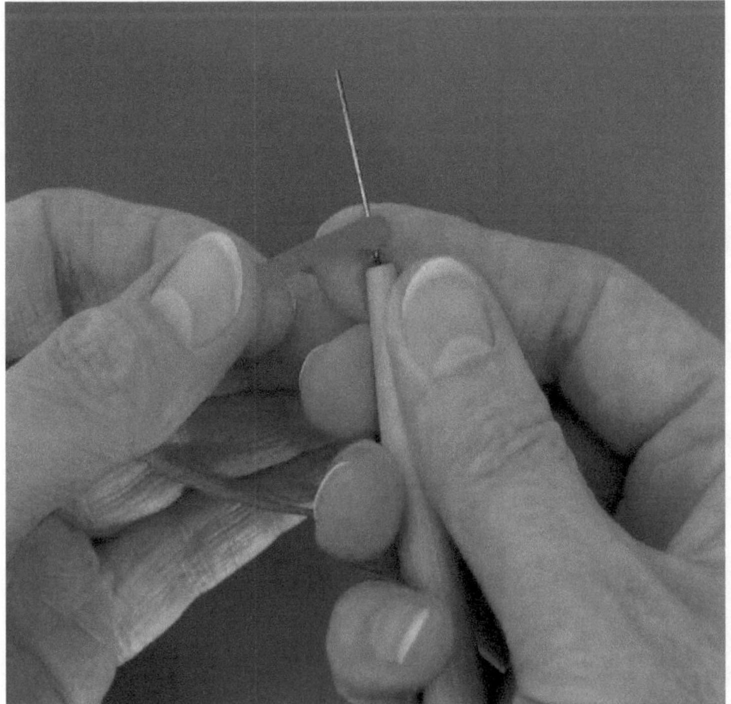

To roll a loop with a needle device: Dampen fingers and bend one finish of a strip over the needle. Roll the strip around the needle with the thumb and pointer of whichever hand feels generally great, applying even, firm weight, while holding the handle of the device with the other hand. Make certain to roll the paper, not the apparatus.

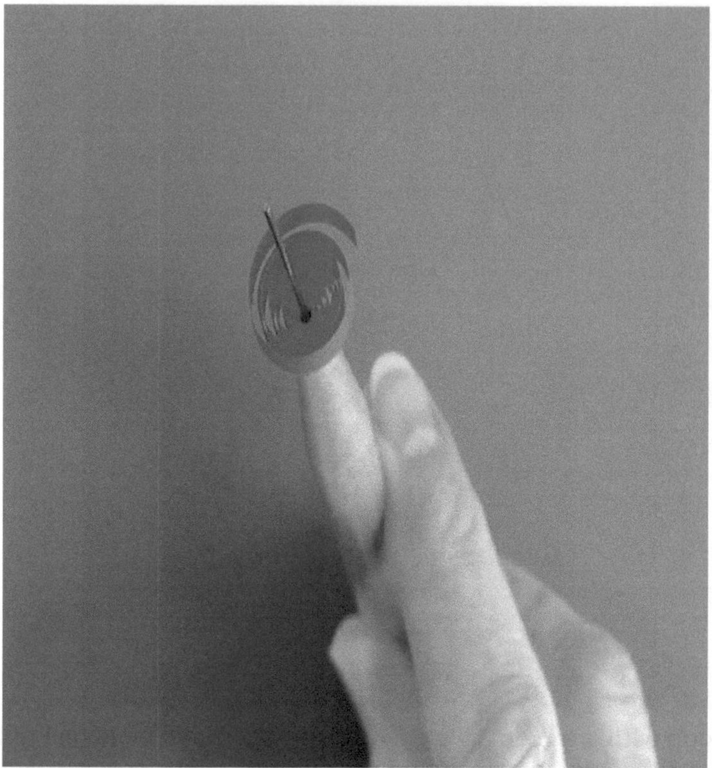

In the case of utilizing an opened instrument or needle apparatus, when the strip is completely rolled, permit the loop to unwind, slide it off the device, and glue the end. Utilize just an exceptionally modest quantity of glue, applying it with the tip of a T-pin, paper penetrating apparatus, or toothpick. Hold the end set up for a couple of seconds while the glue dries. This is known as a free curl, and it's the fundamental shape from which numerous different shapes are made.

CANDY JAR PROJECT

Materials:

Glass container

Grosgrain lace – red, 3/8″

Quilling paper, red, 1/8″

Cardstock, white

Cement froth dabs

Guidelines

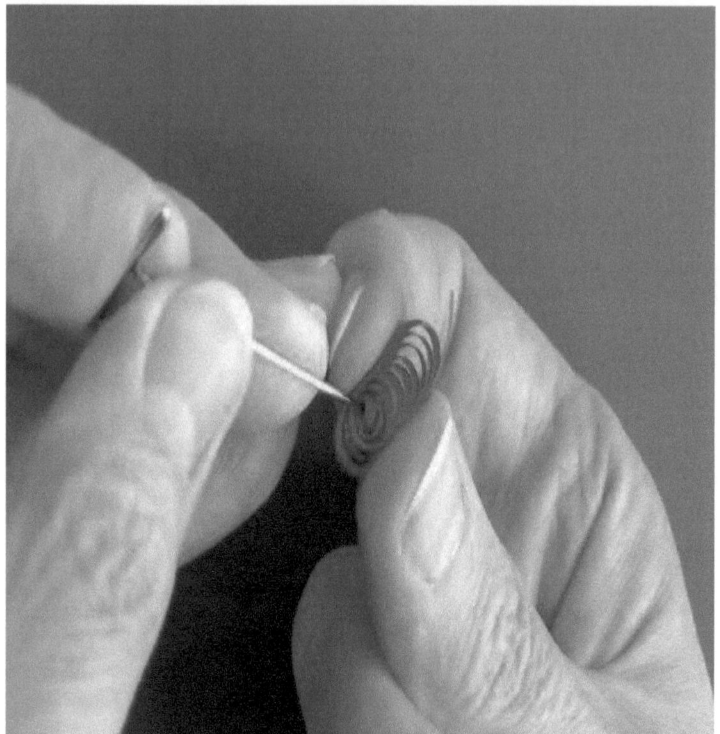

Stage 1: Make 4 tear. Roll a 12″ free curl. Press the curl somewhat between your fingers, and, if fundamental, utilize a pin to organize the inward loops so they are equally dispersed.

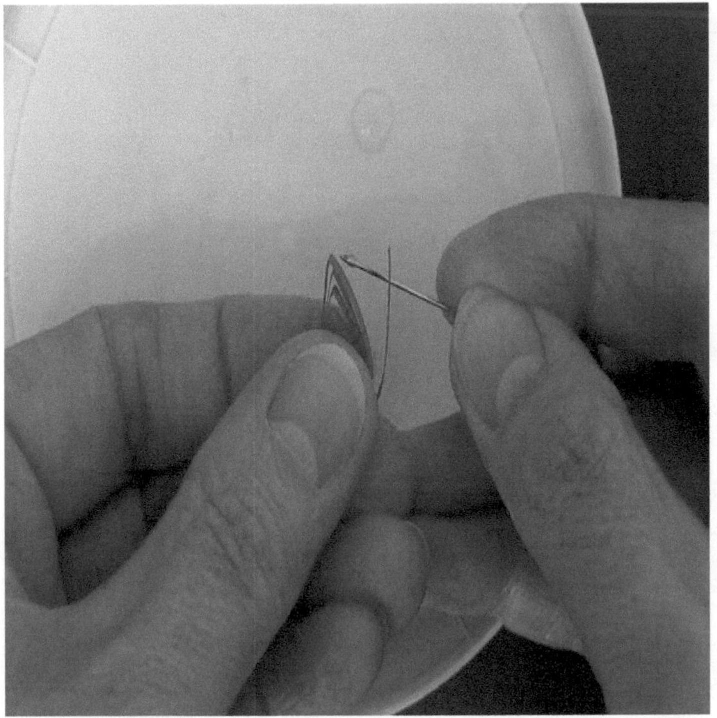

Squeeze strongly at the tip to come to a meaningful conclusion. Glue the end and trim the surplus paper.

Stage 2: Make 2 hearts. Spot 2 tears next to each other on the work board to make a heart shape, situating them in inverse headings so the inward loops seem to meet. Apply stick at the join spot.

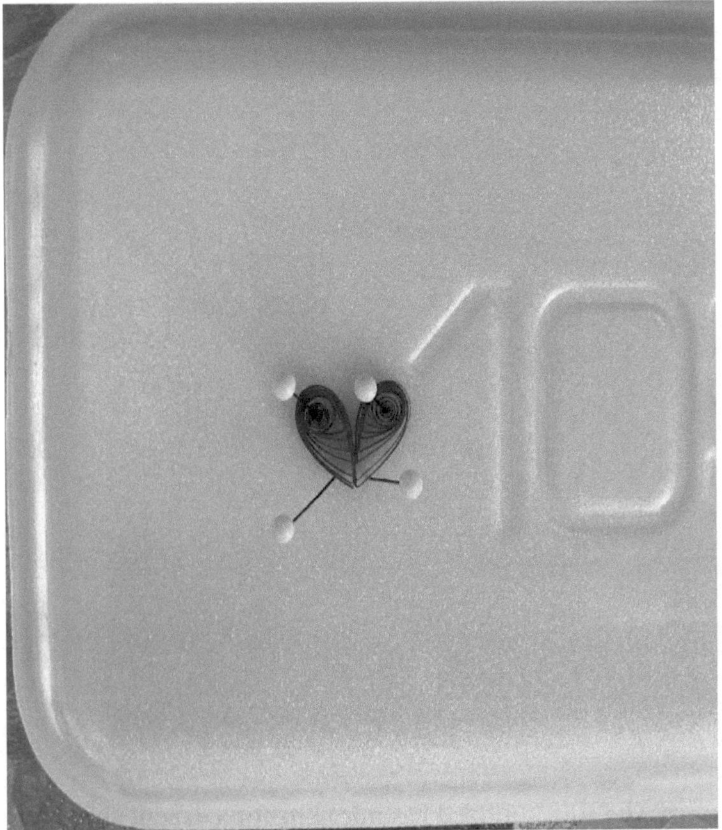

Hold the tears set up with pins while the glue dries.

Stage 3: Fill a container with your preferred treat and tie a lace around it.

Stage 4: Cut 2 white, 1″ cardstock squares and glue a heart on each.

Tip: When sticking a quilled object on a background, spread a shallow puddle of glue on a plastic holder cover or a sheet of waxed paper. Hold the quilling with tweezers and plunge its underside tenderly in stick. Spot legitimately on the background.

Stage 5: Attach 1 square to every strip tail with a glue spot.

VALENTINE CARD

Materials:

Cardstock, red The sort I utilized has mica bits for a decent shimmer.

Watercolor computerized paper Free advanced paper pack

Printer quilling paper, red, 1/8″

Twill tape, white, 1/2″

Paper cut, red

Adornments pincers, 2 level nose

Hop rings, 2 silver

Clear message sticker

Glue stick

Paper shaper

Printer

Guidelines

Stage 1: Score and overlap a 7½"x5½" bit of red cardstock to make a 3¾"x5½" card.

Stage 2: Print out the computerized watercolor background and slice it to quantify 3¼"x5″. Utilize a glue stick to hold fast the square shape to the focal point of the card.

Stage 3: Outline the designed paper with quilling strips. Cover the strips unequivocally at the corners or miter at an inclination as appeared, following my instructional exercise.

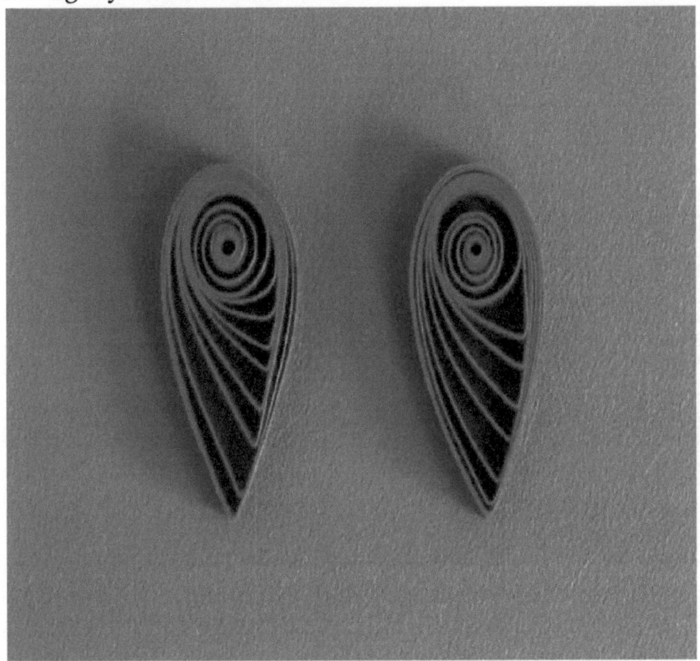

Stage 4: Make a heart (2 tears). Every tear requires a full-length strip, 24″. Position the tears with the goal that the internal loops face a similar way. (This is inverse of the manner in which the sweets container tears were situated.) Facing the curls a similar way will give a decent look when forming the bend. Glue the tears one next to the other, nailing them set up to the work board until dry.

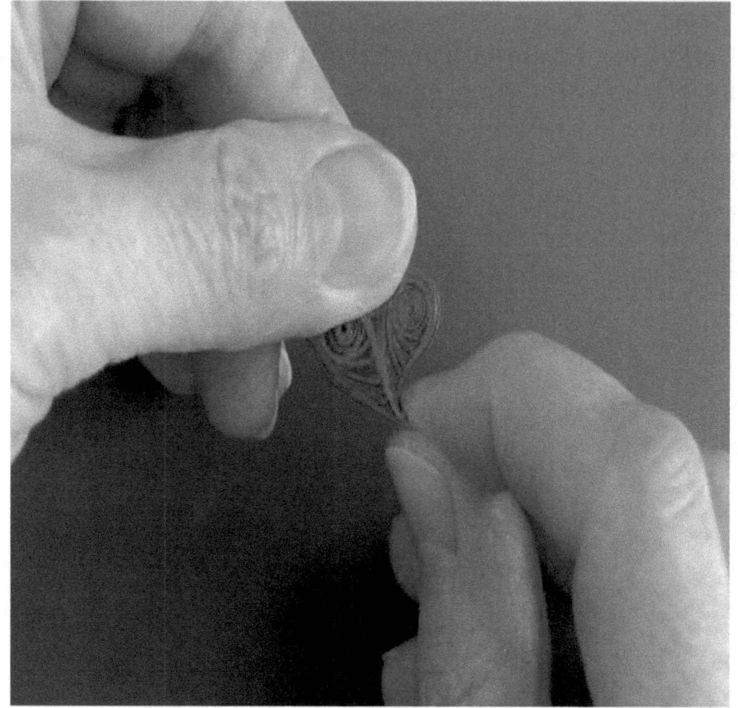

Stage 5: Grasp the tip of the heart and bend it tenderly.

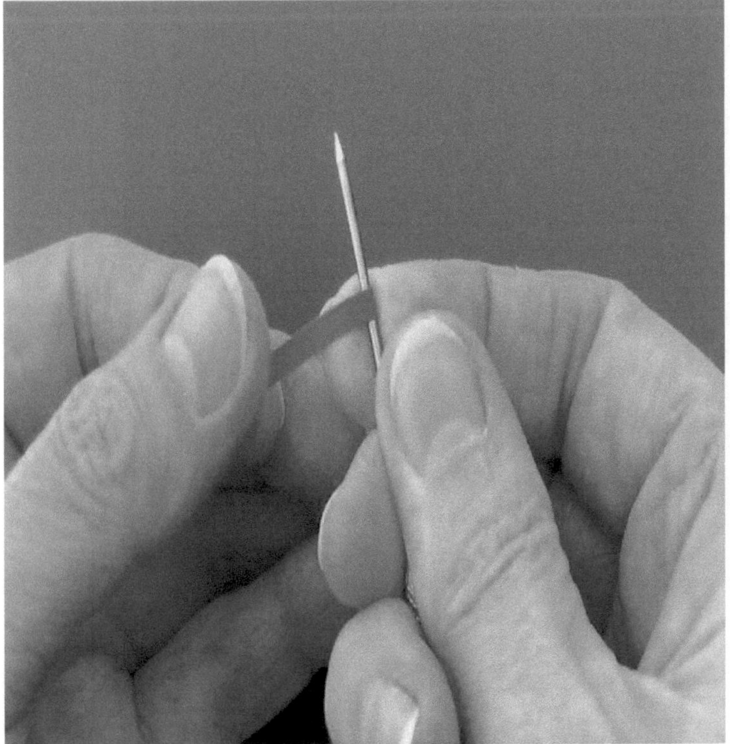

Stage 6: Roll a 2½" strip around the pole of a paper puncturing instrument or round toothpick to make a dot. Glue the torn end.

Tip: A torn end mixes superior to a dull cut.

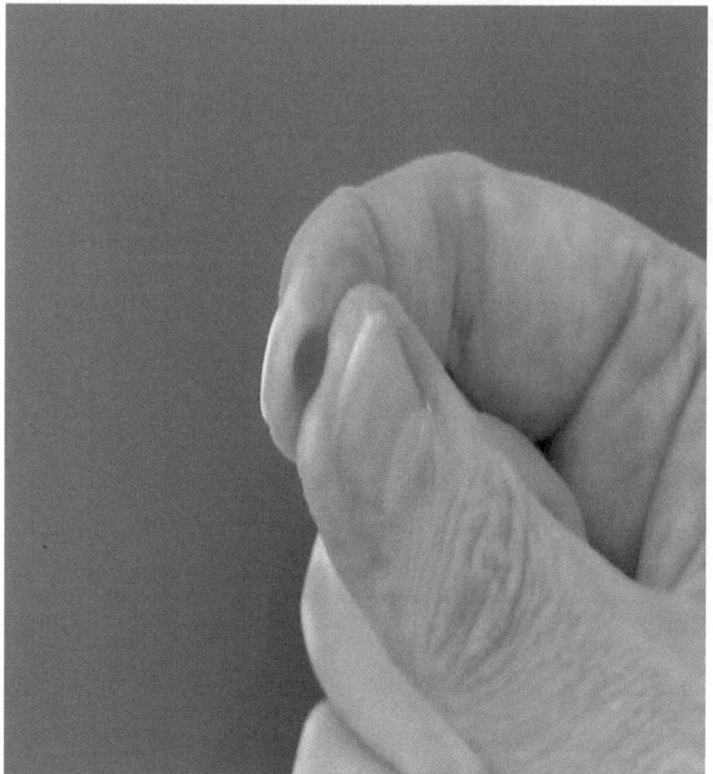

Stage 7: Pinch the dab to frame an oval ring loop.

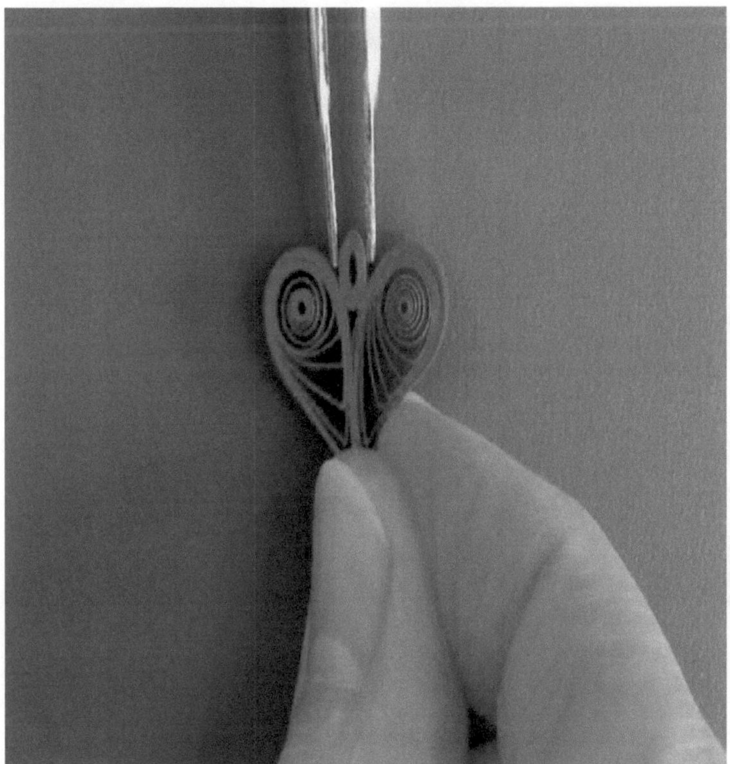

Glue the dab between the heart bends.

Stage 8: Use forceps to open 2 bounce rings and connect them to the ring curl.

Stage 9: Slip the bounce ring onto the paper cut.

Stage 10: Cut a ¾"- wide portion of cardstock to fit the width of the card between the circumscribed edges, and glue it set up, covering the lettering on the printed advanced paper.

Step11: Cut twill tape to a similar length as the cardstock strip. Slide the paper cut/heart onto the twill tape. Focus and glue the twill tape onto the cardstock strip.

Stage 12: Press on an unmistakable sticker message. I utilized "Praise"; within message could peruse "our adoration" or "with the one you love." And obviously, Happy Valentine's Day!

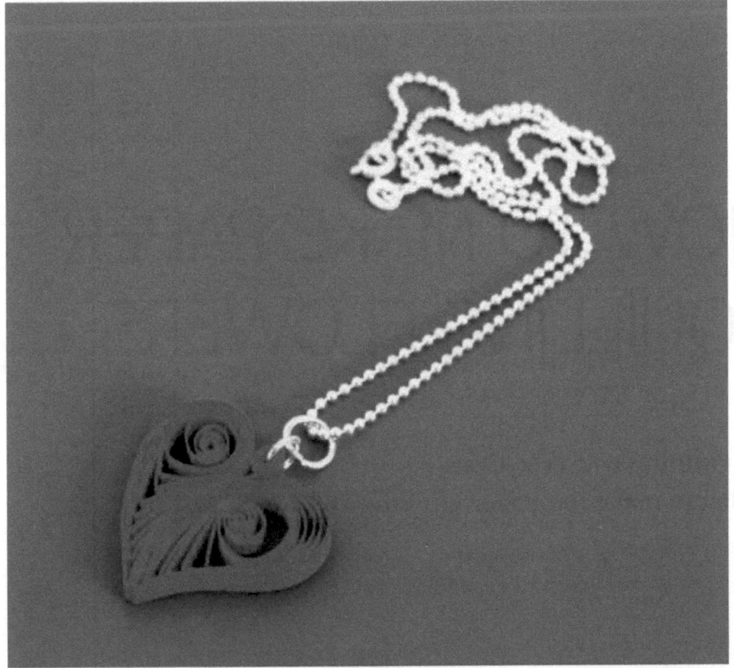

As a variety, include a chain and wear the quilled heart as an accessory pendant. Whenever wanted, splash the heart with a glossy silk finish acrylic stain to give it water opposition and additional toughness.

CHAPTER THREE

HOW TO MAKE PAPER QUILLING FLOWERS

DIY Paper Quilling Fall Tree Craft

Supply list to make the Paper Quilling Fall Tree Craft

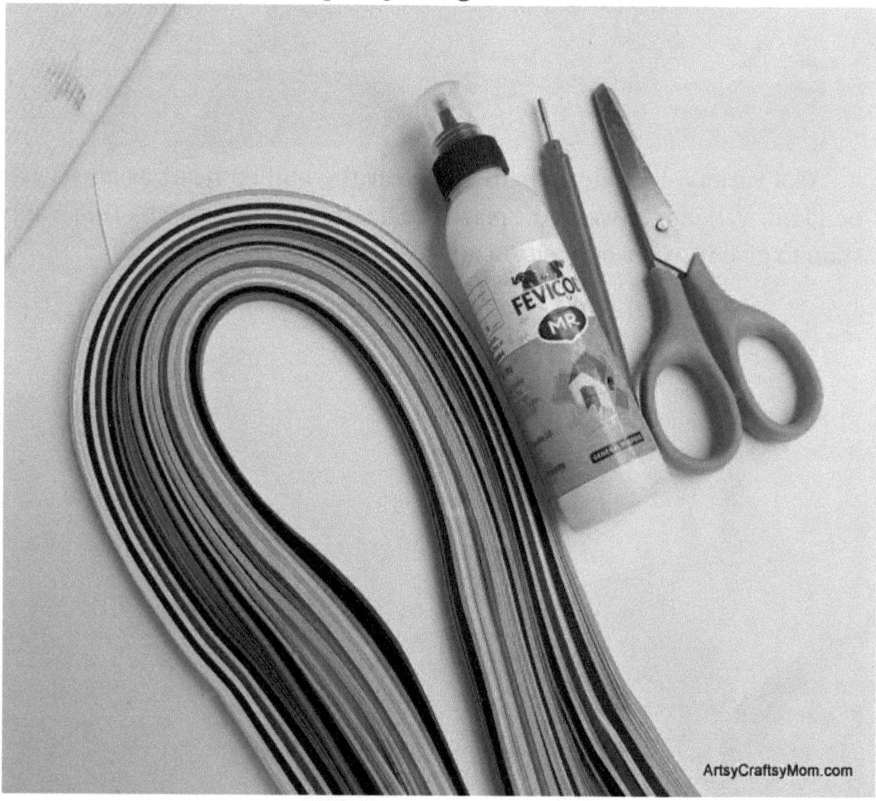

1. Quilling paper strips – 5mm – Red, Yellow, Orange, Brown
2. White cardstock 6 x 12 inches

3. Craft glue
4. Slotted quilling device
5. Scissors

Guidelines to make the Paper Quilling Fall Tree Craft

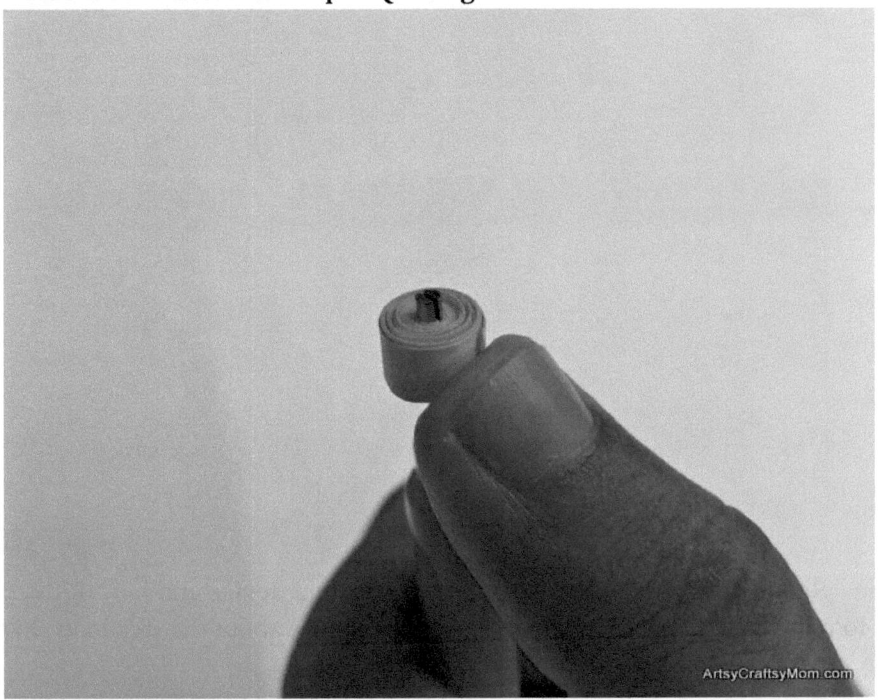

Select 3-4 fall shaded quilling strips. Take a 10-inch long quilling strip and loop the whole strip with the assistance of the opened quilling device.

Remove from wound strip out of the opened device and permit the curl to relax up a bit. Glue the open end to make sure about the free loop shape.

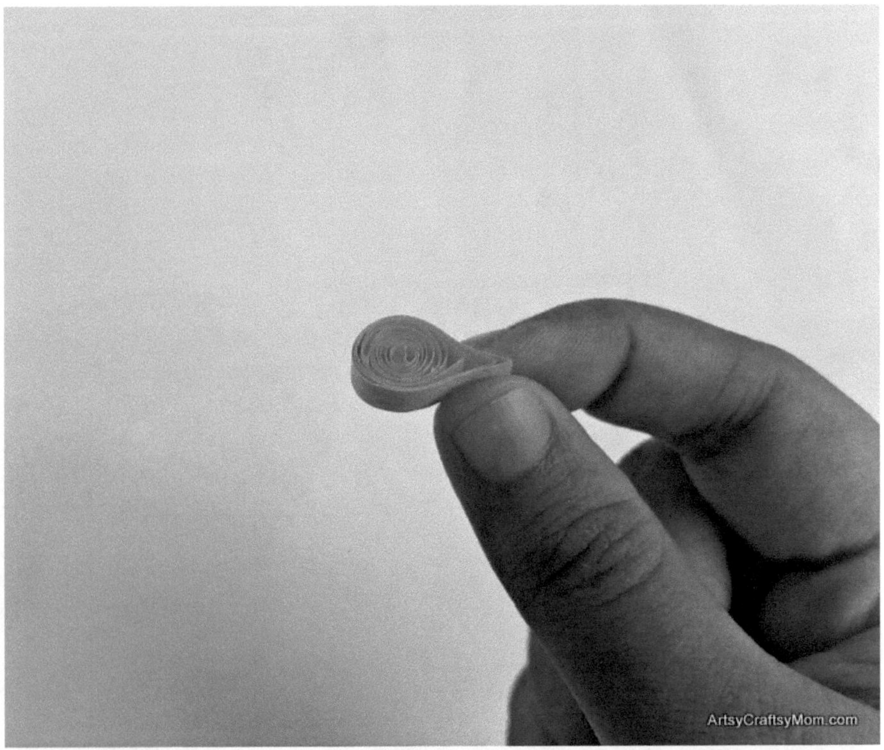

Press any one side of the free curl arranged in the past advance to make a tear shape. We have made a tear shape.

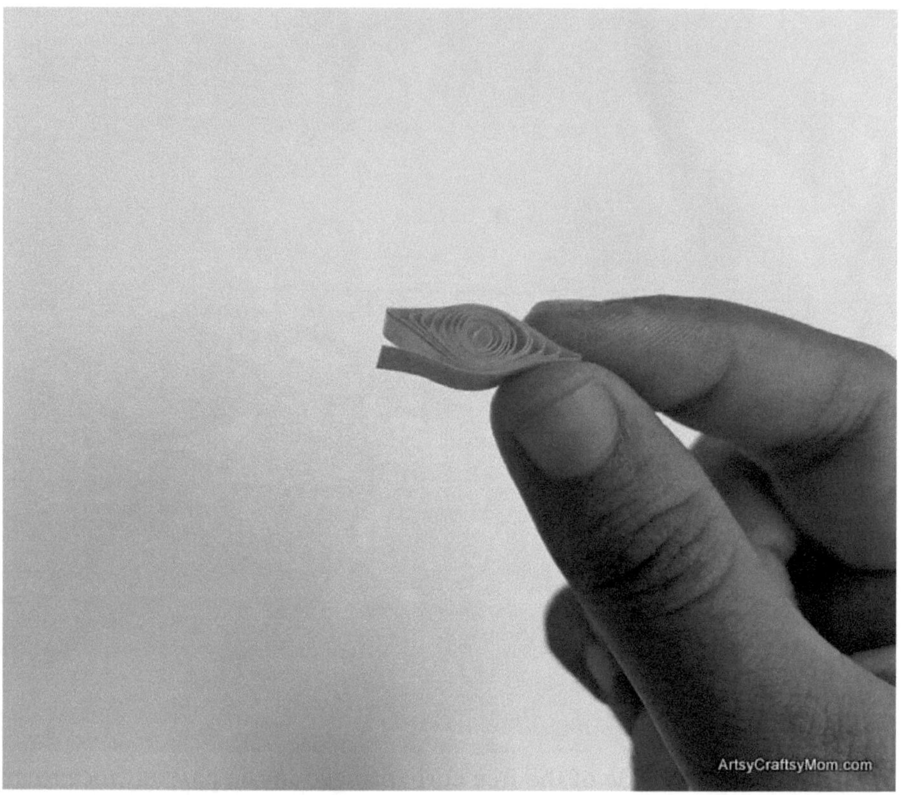

Presently press the contrary side of the loops' recently squeezed side to make a fundamental eye shape. Glue the open finish of the strip to make sure about the shape.

So also, make more essential eye shapes utilizing fall colored quilling strips. These will be the leaves.

Take earthy colored quilling strips and cut them into any altered size you need, mine were 5 inches in length. Utilize the opened instrument to loop around 1 or 1.5 crawls of the strip from any one end.

So also, get ready 6 to 8 additional strips as set up in the past advance.

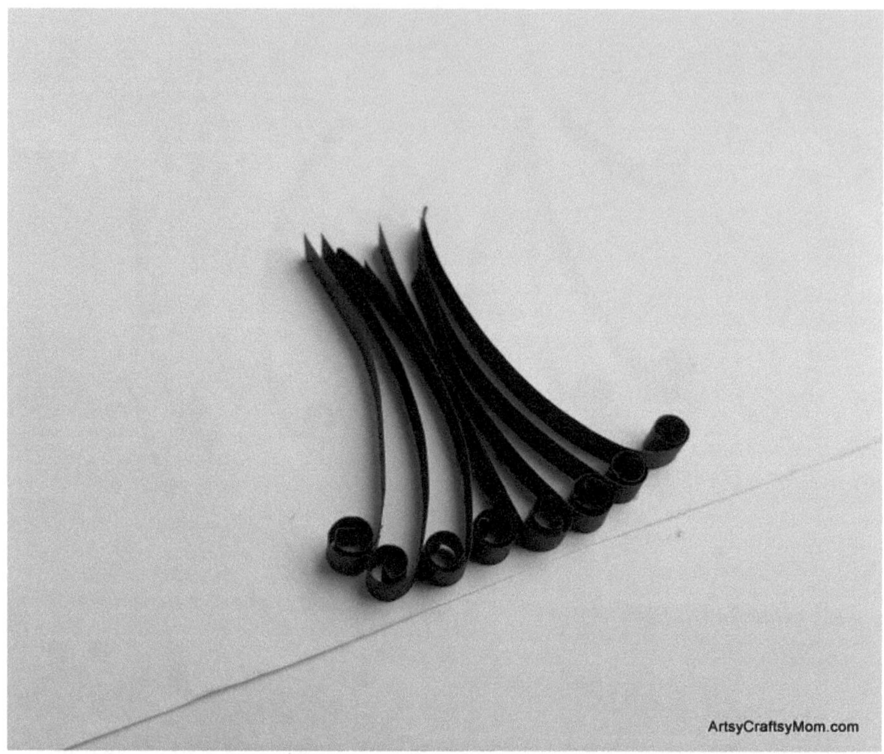

Overlap a bit of white cardstock paper into equal parts to shape a card.. Glue the strips arranged in sync 7 on the paper; fundamentally making the storage compartment of the tree.

Presently take the essential eye shapes (leaves) and begin to stick them over the storage compartment design.

While staying the leaf shapes attempt to keep a pleasant example mix. I stuck 3 to 4 fundamental eye shapes in gatherings.

All done? You can stop once you are happy with the tree design. Permit the glue to dry.

What's more, done!

Paper Quilled Snowflake Ornaments

Materials

- Paper quilling strips 5mm wide and 54cm long – White , Blue
- Quilling opened instrument or a toothpick with a space cut at the back.
- Glue
- Scissors
- Plastic sheet/oil verification paper
- Pencil
- Geometric compass
- White piece of paper
- Small ruler

Instructions to make your Paper Quilled Snowflake Ornaments

1. The initial step is to distinguish the length of the strips for your quilled snowflakes. We have utilized the full length, the half and the quarter length.

2. Using a compass, draw a 5 cm hover or circle on the white sheet. This will be the base of our structure.

3. Next, isolate the hover into 6 equivalent parts and draw your structure. We utilized 3 fundamental quilling folds to make the snowflake – Tight Coil, Teardrop and Marquis

4. For the main crease – Tight Coil, roll a strip around an opened instrument firmly. Glue the end immovably set up

5. For the subsequent overlay or fold – Teardrop, roll a strip around an opened apparatus firmly. Delicately remove it from the apparatus, let it grow between two fingers. Presently with the other hand, marginally squeeze one end to frame a leaf or a tear like structure. Glue the end solidly set up

6. For the third overlay – The marquis or the eye, roll a strip around an opened instrument firmly. Tenderly remove it from the apparatus, let it grow between two fingers. Presently with two hands, somewhat squeeze the two closures to shape an eye like structure. Glue the end immovably set up

7. For the snowflake we need

- 6 full length marquis in white,
- 6 full length tears in blue,
- 6 full length tight loops in white,
- 1 half-length tight loop in white,
- 6 half-length tight loops in blue,
- 18 quarter-length tight curls in blue and
- 6 quarter-length marquis in white.

We wrapped a quarter-length strip around a portion of the pieces to make our structure prettier.

8. We are prepared to collect. Spot the drawing under an OHP sheet and begin gathering each piece from the inside out. First the white half close curl. Stick the blue quarter loops around it. At that point stick the tears utilizing the drawing underneath as reference. The white marquis in the middle of lastly the tears and small scale marquis at the closures. You could make your own plan truly, there is no content here. We made three snowflakes all utilizing similar folds.

9. Let it dry totally with the goal that each fold is adhered solidly to the one close to it. You could cover it modge podge or splash an unmistakable stain over it, however that is redundant.

10. String a few bread cooks twine and you have a little snowflake decorating your Christmas tree.

Paper Quilled Teardrop Vase

Paper Quilled Teardrop Vase

This instructional exercise will tell you the best way to utilize the procedure of quilling to brighten a container in a basic however powerful manner, with paper tears in a slope of colors. You don't have to have done quilling previously, so this is an extraordinary starters venture, and the devices/materials are modest.

What you willl need:

- A container: I utilized a just molded bud jar in artistic, which worked truly well. You need a misty jar, not very enormous, that has no extraordinary curves...only smooth and delicate bends.

- Paper strips in a slope of colors: Search Ebay/Amazon or a paper make shop and you'll discover sets of paper strips sold inexpensively in an immense range of colors. You'll just need one set for a little container like mine.

(Or then again you can make your own in the event that you have a guillotine.)

- Glue: Must have the option to adhere paper to clay. I utilized Aleene's cheap glue.

- Quilling opened instrument: This is a pole with a space toward the end essentially and is modest to purchase.

- Quilling needle instrument: You could utilize a mixed drink stick rather, or anything with a point that can apply stick precisely.

- Quilling board (discretionary): Very helpful to have so you can ensure the tears are a similar size. Could utilize a ruler rather however, or simply draw a hover on a bit of paper to use as a guide!

Helpful to have: Tweezers for moving fiddly things, and cotton buds to clear up stray glue.

Stage 1: Roll the Paper Spirals

Beginning with the most obscure shade of paper you are going to utilize, put the finish of one paper strip into the opened device.

You need to turn the apparatus while holding the paper strip so the paper wraps firmly around the metal pole.

It's not imperative, however the paper strips have one smoother side and one harsher side, so attempt and keep the smoother side outwardly of the winding.

As you pivot the apparatus, keep the framing winding laying on a finger to control it and shield it from getting free or getting into a wreck.

When you have made the entire strip into a loop, placed the curl into a hover on the quilling board and let it gradually spread out to fill the opening molded guide. I utilized the third gap down which is 17mm over.

On the off chance that you don't have a quilling board, you could utilize a drawn circle manage or a ruler and painstakingly let the loop become looser until it gets to the size you need.

At that point you have to put a smidgen of glue toward the finish of the paper strip, within, to hold the curl in that shape. You can utilize a quilling needle or mixed drink stick to apply the glue precisely.

Stage 2: Form the Teardrops

You have to take every one of the curls you make and afterward transform them into tear shapes.

This is remarkably simple and you should simply delicately crush half of the loop between your finger and thumb, and squeeze one end to make a sharp overlay.

It's up to your what sizes you make your tears and relies generally upon the size of your container. I made 4 columns of one size and afterward made tears of a littler size for the top line.

Stage 3: Add the Teardrops to the Vase

Make a modest bunch of quilled tears to begin you off. At that point begin sticking them to your container, beginning from the base.

Simply apply a little glue to the back (principally at the top and the base), and hold the tear onto the jar surface for a brief timeframe. It should stick before long.

When you have finished one line, you can replicate the entirety of the means with an alternate shading and make the following column. And afterward simply Replicate this the entirety of the path up your jar or until you need the plan to wrap up.

I completed 5 columns and halted before the container began to bend outwards at the top. Inward bends like that are difficult to design however it tends to be finished utilizing littler quilled shapes.

Stage 4: Finished!

You have now completed your pretty quilled container!

Much obliged for perusing my instructional exercise, and I trust you discovered this task enjoyable to do :)

Stage 5:

You could also check out videos for quilling for beginners, just incase you love video tutorials.

CHAPTER FOUR

Paper Quilling Flower Basket Project

We are (still!) about paper quilling around here! My tween is fixated and I'm cherishing every last bit of her paper quilled manifestations. We've just mutual a variant of these Paper Quilled Flowers when we made a Paper Quilled Frame out of them prior this year and today we are sharing this sweetheart Paper Quilling Flower Basket Project. My girl is presently chipping away at an adaptation of this undertaking to go into our State Fair and these quilled paper extends additionally make brilliant blessing thoughts. I have a few of them that my little girl has made holding tight my office divider!

On the off chance that you are searching for a task to do along with your children OR for an incredible blessing thought for tweens/adolescents then you should think about getting them a Paper Quilling Kit. We have had a good time with our own and we are continually adding to our quilling supplies!

Supplies You Will Need:

1. Quilling paper strips
2. White fixed paper
3. Craft glue
4. Slotted quilling device
5. Scissors

FEVICOL
MR
FABER-CASTELL
sheSAVED

FEVICOL
MR
GENERAL PURPOSE
sheSAVED

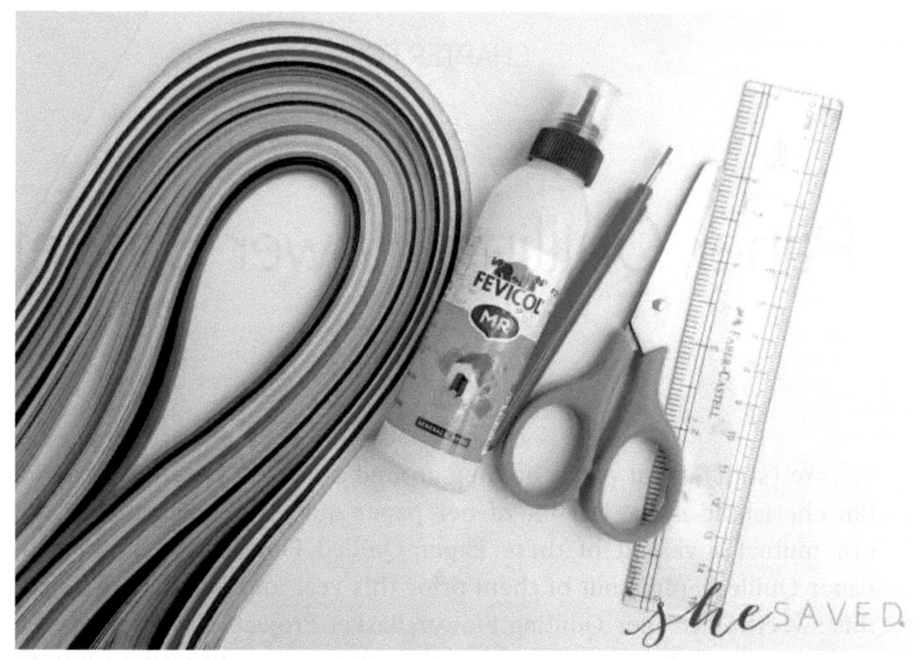

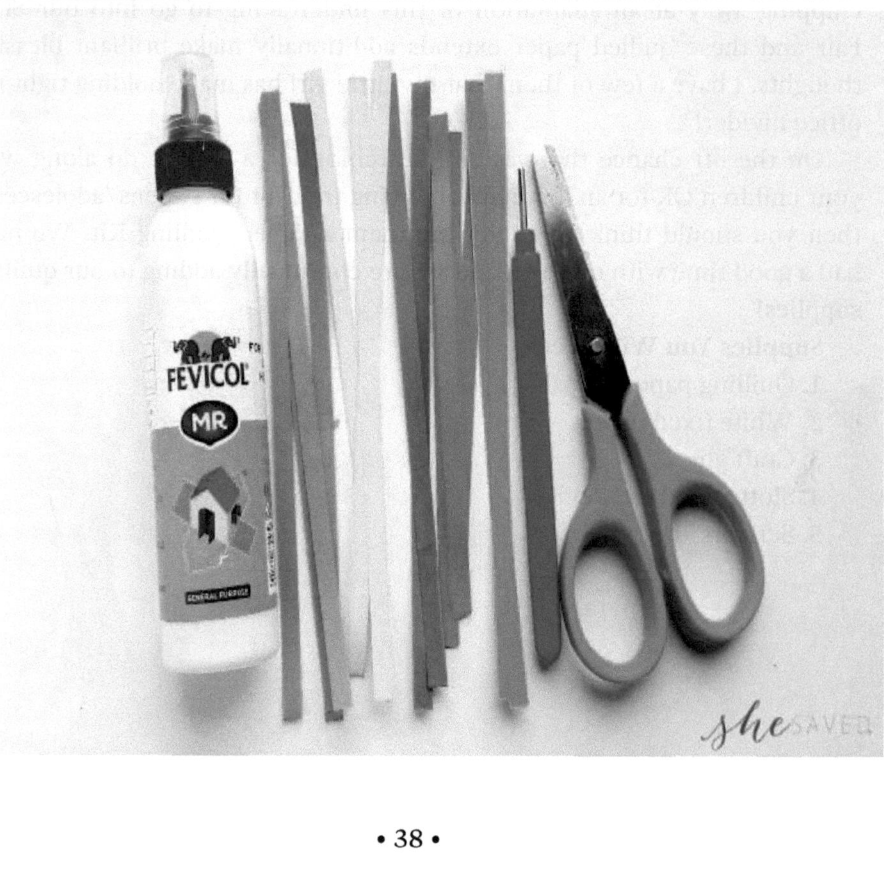

Guidelines for Paper Quilling Flower Basket:

Stage ONE

Take a 10 inches in length quilling strip and curl the whole piece utilizing the opened quilling instrument.

Stage TWO

Remove from snaked strip out of the instrument cautiously.

Stage THREE

Permit the curl to extricate up a piece without anyone else.

Stage FOUR

Press any one side of the free curl to frame a tear shape. Glue the open finish of the strip to make sure about the shape.

Stage FIVE

Also make more tear shapes. For each flower we'll be utilizing 6 tear shapes.

Stage SIX

Presently take a green colored quilling strip and make a free loop with it.

Stage SEVEN

Press any one side of the free loop.

Stage EIGHT

Press the contrary side of the recently squeezed side of the free curl to frame an essential eye shape. Glue the open finish of the strip to make sure about the shape.

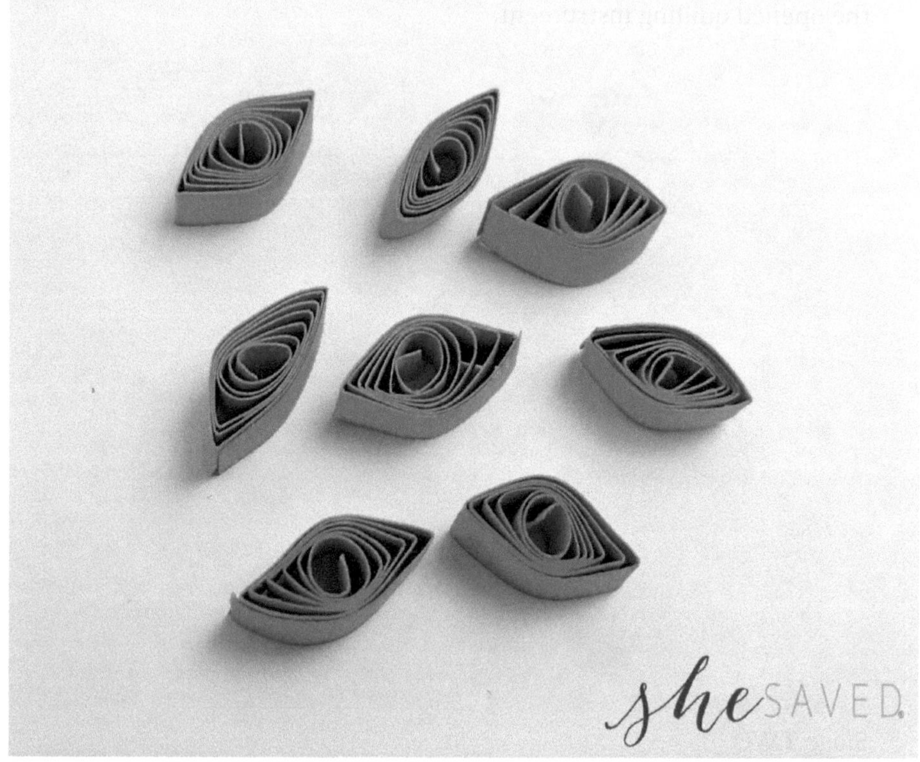

Stage NINE

Essentially make more fundamental eye shapes for the leaves. Utilize green shaded strips.

Stage TEN

Utilize yellow colored strip to make semi-free loops; Create 1 for each flower.

Stage ELEVEN

Take earthy colored strip to make free loops. These earthy colored shaded free loops will be utilized to make the container design.

Stage TWELVE

All shapes prepared? Take a bit of white fixed paper; accumulate all the readied strips and specialty stick.

Stage THIRTEEN

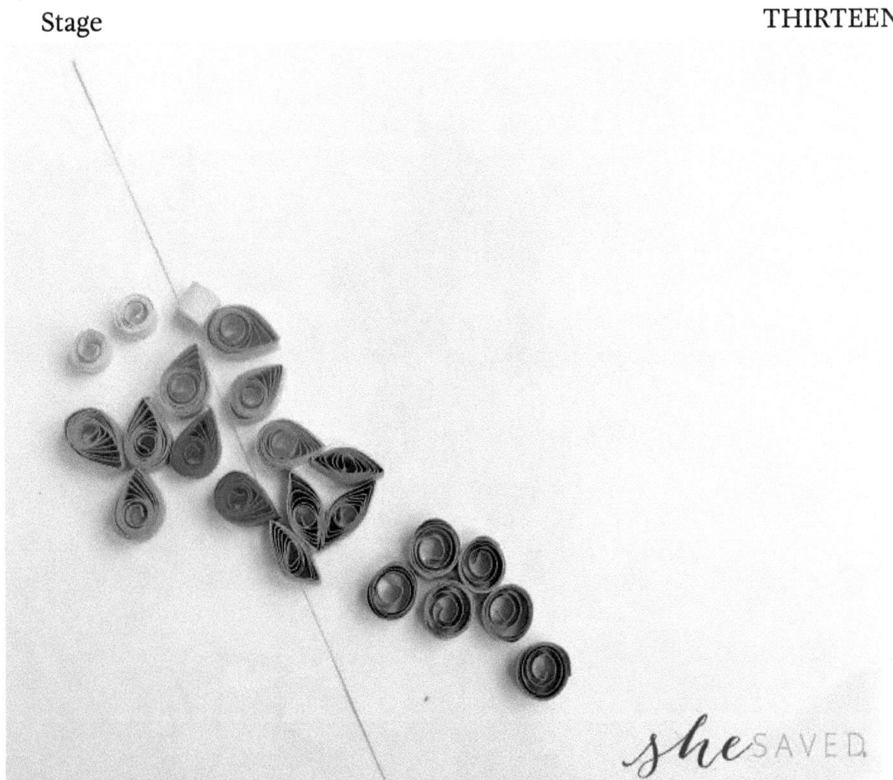

To make the bloom design stick 1 yellow semi-free curl and afterward stick any 6 tear shapes around the loop to finish the flower design.

Stage FOURTEEN

Make the other bloom designs; keep the flowers nearby one another. I made 3 flowers on the base column and 2 flowers on the top line.

Stage FIFTEEN

Glue the leaf designs in the middle of the flower designs; Use the earthy colored free loop examples to make the bin.

Stage SIXTEEN

You can utilize little loop examples to fill the holes between the flowers and the leaves. Include some other subtleties as you wish.

Permit the glue to dry and done! These great paper quilled ventures are slick to outline and furthermore a pleasant method to make hand crafted welcoming cards, simply stick your undertaking to the front of a clear card.

Guidelines on How to Make Easy Quilling Angels for Kids

Rundown: Are you keen on quilling paper makes? On the off chance that truly, you are entirely fortunate here. I figure you may get a few motivations from the present Pandahall instructional exercise on the best way to make simple quilling heavenly attendants for kids.

As I would see it, simple quilling designs are decent decisions for crafts making novices. So I am extremely glad to share you a simple Pandahall instructional exercise about how to make quilling heavenly attendants. Do you anticipate it? I surmise you may get some novel thoughts from it. Presently, how about we begin to see together!

Materials required for the simple quilling angel：

5mm yellow, pink and white quilling paper

scissors
moving pen
white glue

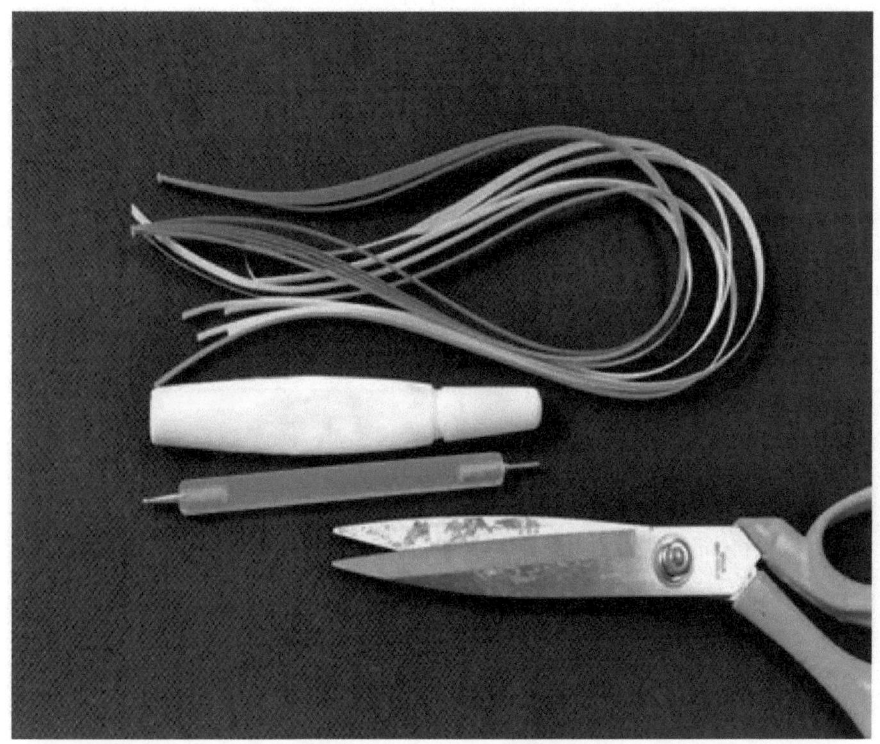

Enter Caption

Stage 1: Make the top of the quilling angel

You simply need to roll a bit of white quilling paper as round shape with moving pen.

Step 2：produce the wings of the quilling angel for the young ones

first, warp a bit of white quilling paper as wing shape thereafter use white glue to glue it.

secondly, warp a small amount of yellow quilling paper as wing shape, and thereafter use white glue to glue it.

third, consolidate the prepared white and yellow quilling paper along with white glue;

fourth, make another wing in similar ways referenced previously.

Stage 3: Make the tail of the simple quilling angel

first, contort two bits of white quilling paper as wing shapes. At that point fix it with white glue;

second, loop a bit of yellow quilling paper similarly;

third, consolidate the three bits of prepared quilling paper along with white glue. You should ensure put the yellow paper in the center and the two bits of white paper on the privilege and left side independently.

Stage 4: Finish the simple quilling heavenly attendant

first, roll a bit of pink quilling paper as heart shape;

second, glue the pink heart, quilling heavenly attendant's head, wings and tail along with white glue, it would be ideal if you see the image appearing beneath.

Time for the simple quilling angel for kids:

Enter Caption

PAPER QUILLED FLOWER CAKE

Enter Caption

I have been completely enchanted with Anthropologie's current window shows for spring. Do you realize that each Anthropologie has its own store craftsman and show organizer? For each new window show, the stores are totally given a typical subject which they would then be able to decipher in an exceptional manner. For this season it was paper quilled flowers, and the outcomes are amazing! In the event that you haven't been to your local Anthropologie, run, don't walk! You can likewise turn upward #anthrowindows on Instagram to see the assortment. One of my undisputed top choices is this pink and orange excellence at the Greensboro, North Carolina Anthropologie. The colors are unadulterated enchantment and I love the mix of quilling with more customary paper bloom strategies. I don't think about you, yet paper quilling hasn't generally been some tea. However, in little portions, it tends to be dazzling!

We utilized their ravishing window show as motivation for this cake clincher. We made little paper quilled orange sprouts and matched them with some paper kumquat branches. *We'll be posting an instructional exercise for the paper kumquat branches soon, yet meanwhile, we would recommend utilizing genuine kumquats! Quilling can be unpredictable and entangled yet we made basic, fragile flowers to enhance our cake. This cake would be ideal for forthcoming spring wedding or child showers and birthday events!

Instructions to after the rise!

Paper Quilled Flower How-To:

Materials:

- White printer paper
- Yellow paper
- Glue stick
- Scissors or potentially paper shaper

Guidelines:

1. For a bordered focus, cut a little bit of yellow cardstock (1.5 cm X 3 cm) and periphery the edge. Move it up and secure with a touch of paste

2. For the bloom petals, cut 1/4″ segments of printer paper.

3. Roll the strip into a tight curl, let it unroll a piece and secure with a spot of paste.

4. With two fingers, squeeze the round loop at the closures so the shape turns out to be to a greater degree a precious stone.

5. Continue creation the jewel shapes until you have enough petals.

6. To make a twofold jewel petal, make two precious stone loops and crunch them together, making sure about them by folding another segment of paper over the external edge of the two pieces and sticking set up.

7. Glue all your completed petals around the bordered or wound focal point.

Presently take your quilled roses notwithstanding some kumquat branches or other foliage, and enhance your cake!

Paper Quilling Flower Pendant

At the point when I was an adolescent and simply beginning to make my own gems, probably the greatest test I confronted was spending plan. I had a touch of spending space for the non-consumables and the bigger bundles: apparatuses that were reused from venture to extend, huge bundles of jumprings and earwires...

In any case, I battled with things like costly dots that were sold in amounts enormous enough for only one bundle.

I likewise preferred to do things another way. Beaded gems is somewhat cool, yet it's... well, exhausting.

I mean it doesn't need to be (and you can see that inevitably I built up my own style with this wire wrapped gemstone wristband) however I despite everything love adding a measurement to my gems that is new, and utilizing remarkable materials.

In view of this, I have some good times shock seeking you on October eighth – stay tuned! In the event that you need to be advised of updates ensure you're a supporter (it's free)!

Presently, on to this paper quilling bloom pendant.

Paper quilling is a great side interest and the consumable supplies are so moderate! You can utilize bought quilling strips, or make you own, you need to keep up a consistency thus it very well may be dull. Quilling strips come in huge, reasonable bundles so it merits getting them premade.

Obviously, this paper adornments make isn't water safe so you'll need to get it far from water. You can seal it in the event that you'd like utilizing a sealer.

After you're finished making this paper quilling flower pendant, attempt it with different structures. Transform it into keyrings, make littler renditions as studs, and consolidate a couple quilled structures to frame an announcement neckband or wristband.

What you have to make a paper quilling flower pendant:

- Quilling paper strips
- Glue
- quilling opened apparatus
- 4mm fake pearl dab (discretionary)
- Jump ring
- Finished chain or string
- Optional: extra globules to decorate chain

How to make a paper quilling flower pendant:

1. Select a paper strip in your first shading, and utilize the opened quilling instrument to curl the strip.

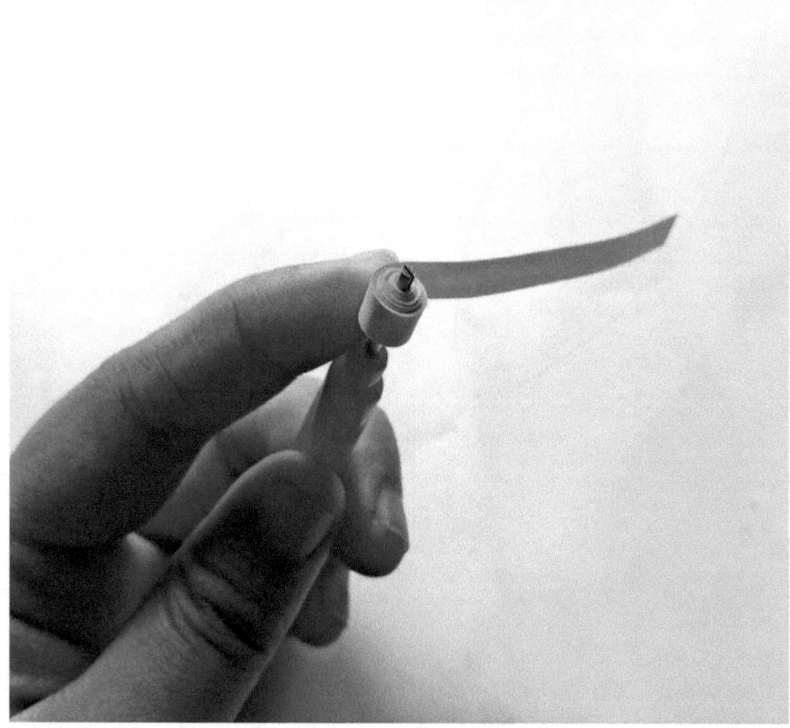

2. Subsequent to curling the whole strip cautiously remove it from the quilling instrument, holding the strip so it doesn't uncoil.

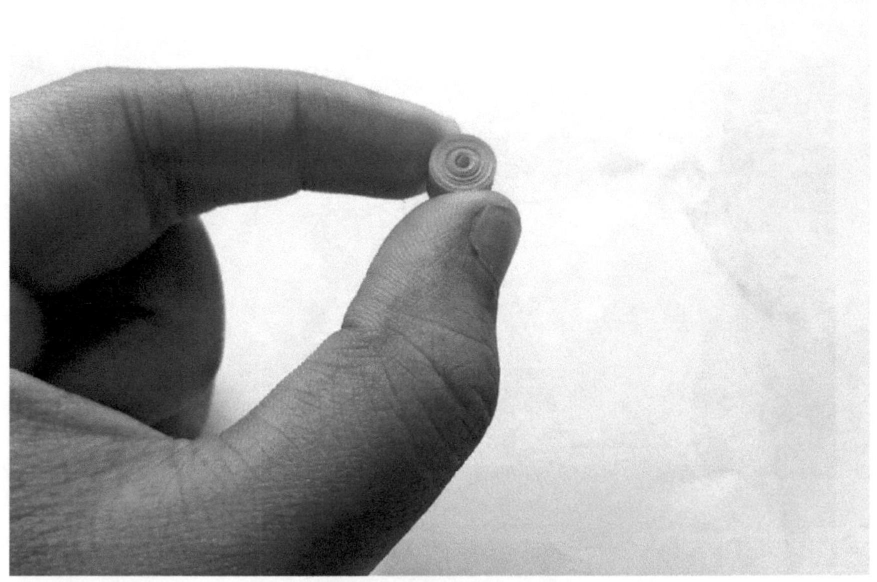

1. Allow the curl to release up a piece.

3. Spot the inexactly looped strip on a level surface and paste a little dot in the focal point of the quilled circle (discretionary).

5. Fix the curl again by holding it between 2 fingers and pulling the open end. When the middle part has fixed, roll the remainder of the strip around it and apply stick at the tip to make sure about your curl. This will be the focal point of the paper quilling bloom.

6. Select a quilling strip in your subsequent shading and quill it utilizing the opened quilling instrument.

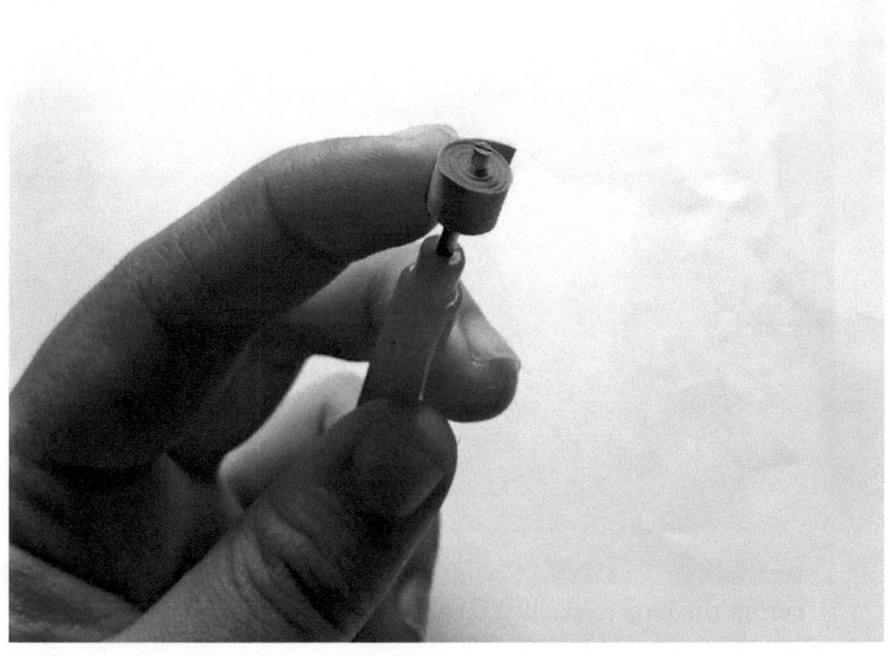

7. In the wake of quilling the strip cautiously remove it from the device.

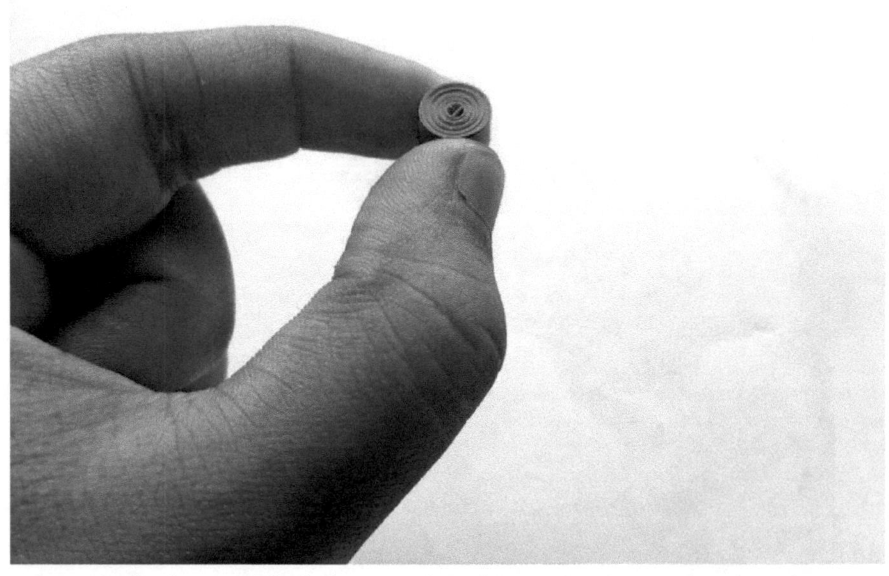

8. Permit the loop to slacken up a piece by setting it on a level surface.

9. Take the freely quilled example and squeeze one side to make a pointy edge. You presently have a tear shape.

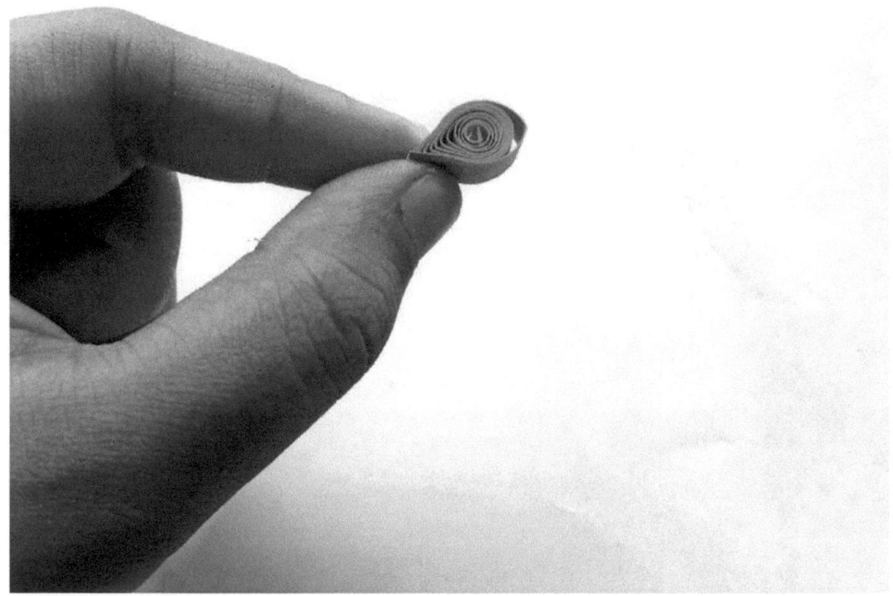

10. Presently squeeze the contrary side of the quilled strip to make another pointy edge. You presently have an eye shape.

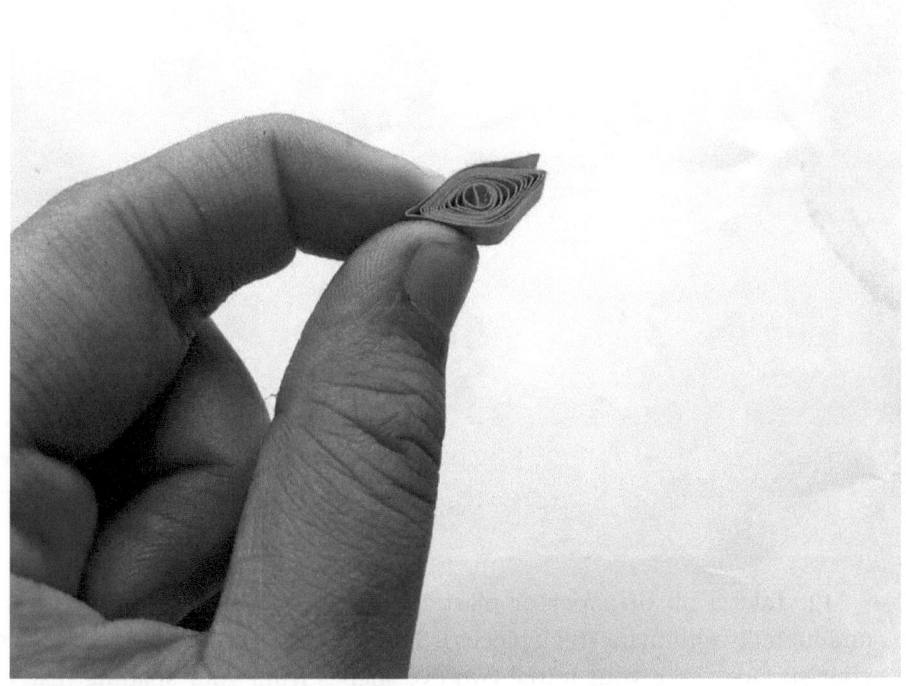

11. Replicate stages 6-10 to make 5 more eye shapes utilizing similar shaded strips for an aggregate of six. Make 3 more eye shapes in your third paper shading.

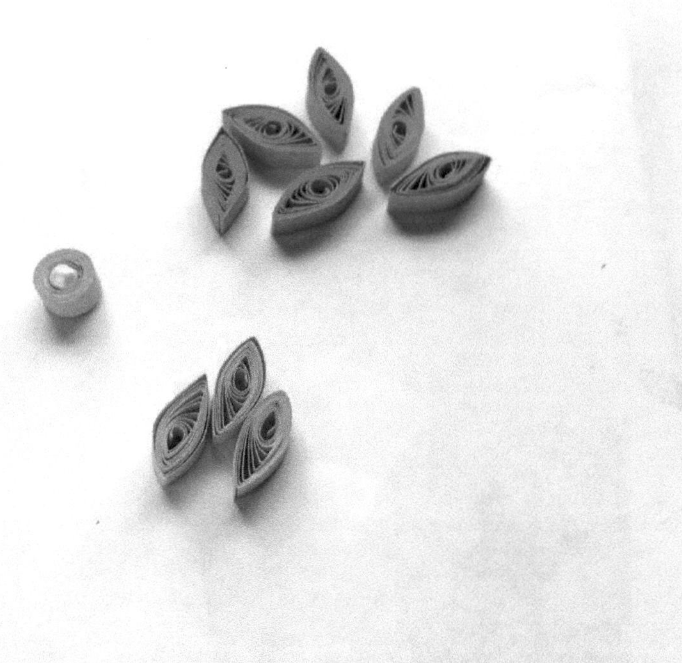

12. Take a bit of paper or plastic with a smooth surface (so you can undoubtedly eliminate stuck pieces). Spot the inside aspect of the bloom on your surface. Take your initial two eye shapes from your shading that you have six of and join them to the circle. Do this by sticking any of the pointy edges to the inside circle. Paste the adjusted aspect of the eye shapes to one another also, interfacing your petals.

13. Presently take one from your second shade of eye-formed loops, and paste it a similar path to the inside and to the bordering petal.

14. Replicate your example until your paper quilling bloom shape is finished.

15. Make a tight curl with a moderately greater circle on the middle.

16. Append the curl to the bloom design between any two of your petals to fill in as a circle. On the off chance that you'd prefer to seal your plan, right now is an ideal opportunity to do as such. Ensure you leave the gap in the curl that you made in sync 15 open.

17. Connect a bounce ring however the circle of the loop to finish the pendant.

18. Connect your jump ring to a line or chain and wear with satisfaction! In the event that you'd prefer to include dots, you'll have to either complete your own chain, or eliminate the finishes that accompanied it and pick huge holed dots as accents.

Wear it and be glad for your paper quilling flower abilities!

DIY Paper Top Is The Perfect Hanukkah Craft!

Enter Caption

DIY turning tops produced using segments of paper and toothpicks! These tops may be close to nothing, however they sure turn, and whenever made effectively, they can turn for a significant long time. What's more, regardless of whether of not they turn well, they sure are incredible looking! So get out the straightforward supplies and have a bit of making fest to end Hanukkah on an inventive note! Prepared, we should get turning!

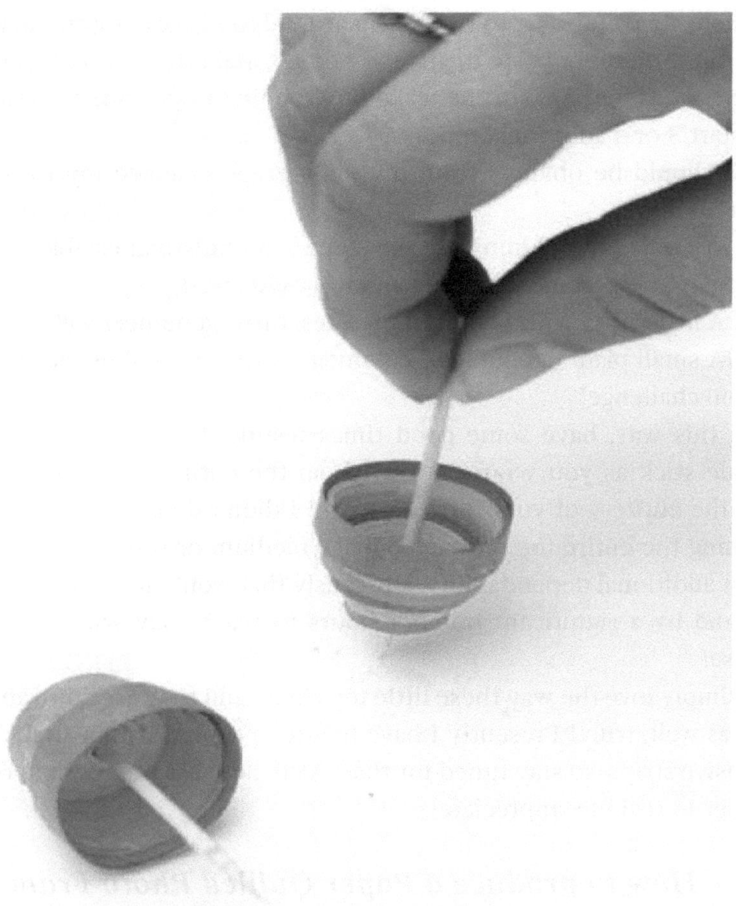

Enter Caption

You'll Need:

• 1/4" paper strips, I cut mine from the length of A4 sheets of shaded cardstock

• toothpicks

• white stick

The most effective method to:

It is remarkably significant that the primary strip is firmly wound onto the toothpick and stuck well. I suggest wrapping only the first round onto numerous toothpicks and giving them a brief period to dry before including ensuing strips. Include a couple of spots of paste to the furthest limit of the main strip and start to twist strip around toothpick, approximately 1/2" from tip. Add more paste to strip as you go, and attempt to keep toothpick as vertical as perhaps. In the wake of wrapping first strip, put aside to dry and start 3 or 4 additional tops.

As should be obvious from my photographs I made my tops in three different ways:

1. A circle: all columns are enveloped by indistinguishable design. the outcomes are incredible looking and top twists well
2. A little plate with ventured up sides: turns genuinely well
3. A small plate (a couple of columns) with ventured up sides: turns the best no challenge!

In this way, have some good times testing, however make a point to include stick as you wrap new strips so the entire top won't breakdown after the entirety of your difficult work! I didn't do this yet would suggest brushing the entire top with decoupage medium or watered down paste to give it additional dependability. Obviously that would imply that you'd need to stand by a significant number hours to really play with them, so you choose!

I simply love the way these little tops look, and they are enjoyable to play with as well, truly! Presently I have to attempt them with a stick and more extensive strips, so stay tuned for that! Also, here is a photograph of our top spinner in real life, appreciate!

How to produce a Paper Quilled Photo Frame

An adorable and in-a-spending blessing thought for your friends and family. Make a quilled paper quilled photograph frame!

Enter Caption

What you need

You need:

1. Froth board
2. X-acto cut and scissor
3. Solid sticky paste and art stick
4. Pencil and ruler
5. Quilling paper

6 Beads.

Guidelines

Step-1: Measure your photograph size and cut out 2 bits of froth board including additional 2 inches both width and length of the photograph size. Draw 1 inch fringe around any one piece and a topsy turvy curve shape directly in the top center aspect of the other piece. See the image. Cut out the casing (the piece with outskirts) as flawlessly as could reasonably be expected. Cut out the curve shape perfectly also.

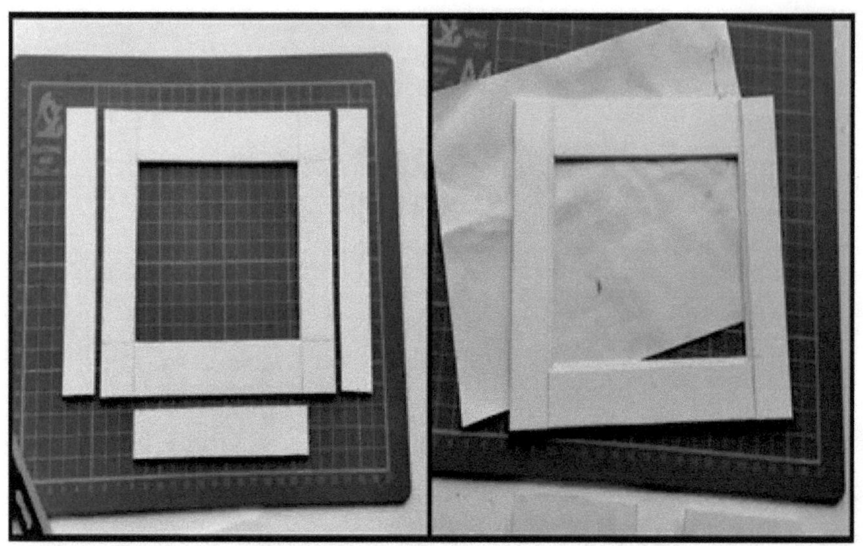

Enter Caption

Step-2: Now place the casing on a plain surface. Measure and cut 3 pieces from the froth board for the sides and base aspect of the froth. Paste the pieces flawlessly along their place. The top side of the casing ought to stay open. This is for inserting the Photograph of the frame

Step-3: Cut out a tie formed example from the froth board for the stand. Make a half cut along the best 1 .5 cm of the stand and twist it. Paste the posterior of the edge and afterward stick the 1.5 cm part of the remain on the rear slantingly by keeping the corner coordinated with the side of the casing.

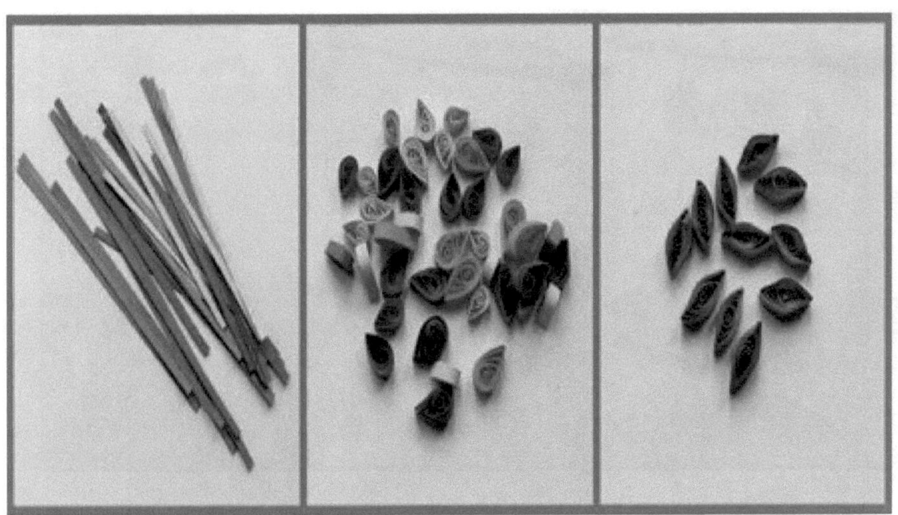

Enter Caption

Step-4: Prepare papers strips for qulling. Utilize splendid colors for the flowers and green for the leaves. Utilize the splendid colored paper strips to make tear molded example. Make the same number of as you have to make flowers. Utilize the green colored paper strips to make leaf molded example. Make the same number of as you need.

Step-5: Place a piece paper under the edge before beginning the paper quilling craftsmanship on the edge. Utilize white/create paste to join the quilled papers. Start to stick the quilled papers from a side of the casing. Just paste and spot them. I utilized 6 tear design for each flower. You may include more petals on the off chance that you need to. Paste more examples to make a chain of flowers.

Enter Caption

Step-6: Create more paper quilling flowers all around the edge. Attempt to keep a pleasant shading mix. Paste the leaves between the flowers. I additionally included some false pearl dots the focal point of the flowers and some free quilled hovers in the little holes.

The End

THE END

Printed by Libri Plureos GmbH in Hamburg,
Germany